I0605776

NORTH AMERICAN
FIELD GUIDES

SEASHELLS

Peggy Snow

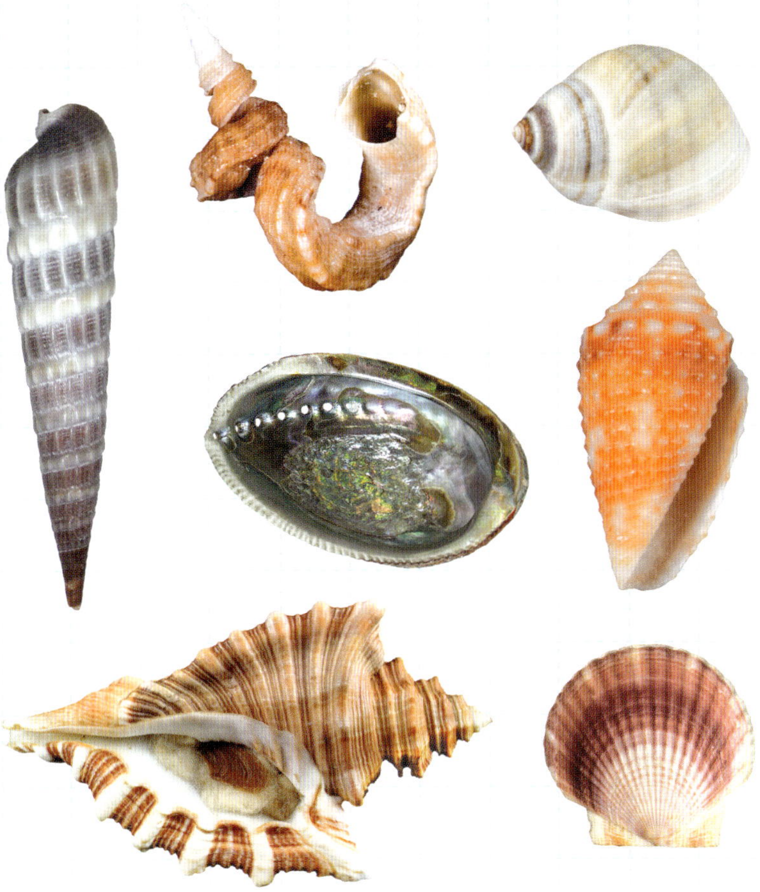

An Imprint of Abdo Reference | abdobooks.com

CONTENTS

WHAT ARE SEASHELLS?

Seashells are the hard outsides of the sea animals known as marine mollusks. Such animals include snails, clams, mussels, oysters, and many more. Most mollusks have shells, but some, such as squids and octopuses, do not. There are about 100,000 known seashells worldwide.

The shell of a mollusk is called an exoskeleton. These sea animals are invertebrates, which means they don't have backbones. Their bodies are soft and spongy, and they need protection. The shell provides protection from predators and support for some organs. The sea creatures are connected to their shells.

Many common seashells are found along the Atlantic and Pacific coasts and throughout the Gulf of Mexico in North America. Seashell animals thrive in salt water.

- Seashells are diverse in shape, color, size, and texture.
- Some seashells have colors that blend with their environment for protection.
- Seashell animals live in mud, sand, or attached to rocks.
- Most seashells come from gastropods or bivalves.
- Gastropods have a single shell called a univalve.
- Bivalves have two shells.

HOW ARE SEASHELLS FORMED?

Seashells are formed from the secretions of the animal.

The mantle is a thin covering of flesh over the body. Cells in the mantle release proteins and minerals to form a shell. The first innermost layer is smooth and shiny. The second layer is chalky. And the outer layer is often rough.

Growth lines are created around the opening as the animal adds to its shell. The process of growing a shell happens slowly. Shells get larger with age to house the growing animal.

- The mantle connects the animal to its shell.
- Shell layers are mostly made of calcium carbonate.
- Mollusks create three layers of shell.

Mollusk bodies have three regions: the head, the foot, and the mass that contains their organs. Some mollusks have a well-developed head, like snails. Others do not, such as clams. The foot muscle is used for moving, digging, and grasping.

HOW DO SEASHELLS END UP ON LAND?

The waves and tides of an ocean bring seashells to the beach. Most are washed up empty because the animal inside has died. Its body decomposed or became food for another sea creature. The empty shell floats in the ocean until a current brings it ashore. Shells can travel thousands of miles. Some are broken down as they are thrown against rocks and sand. They become the tiny grains of the ocean floor or the beach.

HOW TO USE THIS BOOK

Tab shows the seashell family.

The seashell's common name appears here.

PEN SHELLS

SAWTOOTH PEN SHELL

(ATRINA SERRATA)

The sawtooth pen shell is large and elongated. It has closely spaced small scales. They are serrated, like a saw. These shells are wedge-shaped and delicate. More than 30 ribs spre d out from the long, straight hinge. The sawtooth pen s ell is translucent, allowing for light to pass through it. Its nterior is pearl gray to purplish.

This paragraph gives information about the seashell.

SPOT

inches (15.2 to

vish gray to

own

Habitat: In sandy mud

Range: North Carolina to Texas

WHAT ARE PEN SHELLS?

Pen shells are bivalves with a triangular shape and a pointed end. They grow to be long and slender. The shells are typically thin and fragile. Their exterior is covered with rough, spiny ridges, and inside reveals a shiny layer near the tapered end. The sea creature buries the narrow, its shell into sand or mud.

Sidebars provide additional information about the topic.

28

'IFF PEN SHELL *(ATRINA RIGIDA)*

stiff pen shell has 15 to 25 rows of tubular scales. an shape is similar to the sawtooth pen shell. But moderately thick-shelled and fairly strong. The sea ature burrows into their soft bottom habitat, leaving the e edges exposed to water. Stiff pen shells are almost nslucent. The interior is multicolored with hues of orange eir exterior is often partially covered in sea growth, suc algae and sponge animals.

HOW TO SPOT

Size: 5 to 11 inches (12.7 to 27.9 cm)
Color: Dark grayish to olive brown
Habitat: In sandy mud
Range: North Carolina to Texas

FUN FACT

Black pearls are sometimes found in pen shells. They are used to make jewelry.

29

The seashell's scientific name appears here.

How to Spot features give information about the seashell's size, color, habitat, and range.

Fun Facts give interesting information about seashells.

Images show the shell.

BLOOD ARK *(ANADARA OVALIS)*

The blood ark forms a small shell with about 35 ridges, known as ribs. The base color of the shell is neutral but often has a brown fur-like coating, known as the periostracum. The blood ark gets its name from having hemoglobin. This substance gives blood its red color. Very few seashell animals have red blood. A blood ark's body is red. It is native to the United States from the Atlantic Ocean to the Gulf of Mexico.

HOW TO SPOT

Size: 2 inches (5.1 cm)
Color: White or cream with dark brown
Habitat: In sand or mud of shallow water
Range: Massachusetts to Texas

WHAT ARE ARKS?

Ark shells are also called ark clams and belong to the scientific class of bivalves. They have two separate shells connected at a hinge. Arks have boat-shaped interior shells. Their thick exterior protects them from the pounding of strong waves. They are sometimes camouflaged to blend in with stones. There are about 200 species of arks worldwide.

CUT-RIBBED ARK

(ANADARA SECTICOSTATA)

The cut-ribbed ark has deep, curved grooves and ridges that fan out from the hinge. These shells get their name from the faint lines that run across the grooves and ridges in half circles. Their shape is oblong, and the two shells are slightly different in size. The cut-ribbed ark is one of the largest in the ark clam family. The shells are usually covered with dark brown patches near the curved edge.

HOW TO SPOT

Size: Up to 4 inches (10.2 cm)

Color: White with dark brown

Habitat: In sand or mud of shallow water

Range: North Carolina to Texas

FUN FACT

Collecting seashells is a hobby in many parts of the world. A person who collects and studies shells is called a conchologist.

PONDEROUS ARK

(NOETIA PONDEROSA)

The ponderous ark has a heavy, strong shell. There are 27 to 31 ribs with a thin groove in between. One of its notable features is silky black "fur" that covers most or all of the shell. Its shape is long and angular. Numerous "teeth" line the inside hinge. The ponderous ark lives along the eastern and southern coasts of the United States.

HOW TO SPOT

Size: Up to 2.6 inches (6.6 cm)
Color: White with dark brown or black
Habitat: In sand of shallow water
Range: Virginia to Texas

TRANSVERSE ARK

(ANADARA TRANSVERSA)

The transverse ark is small and oblong. Between 30 and 35 ribs fan out from the hinge to the opening. One shell is larger and overlaps the other. The shells are thick with a grayish-brown to dark-brown covering. They are found in shallow waters, sometimes attached to rocks. The transverse ark is very common on island beaches of Florida.

HOW TO SPOT

Size: 1 inch (2.5 cm)
Color: White with brown coating
Habitat: In sandy mud or attached to rocks
Range: Massachusetts to Texas

WHITE-BEARDED ARK

(BARBATIA CANDIDA)

The white-bearded ark shells are roughly oblong in shape. They are connected at a straight hinge. The shells have many ribs that extend from a large bump to their outer edges. Growth ridges cross the ribs, creating small beads. The shells have a brown coating. Thread-like material sticks out from the shell edges, giving it a beard-like appearance. Its dark layer is sometimes worn away by the time the shells reach the shore. The white-bearded ark lives along the southeastern Atlantic coast of the United States to the Gulf of Mexico.

HOW TO SPOT

Size: 1 to 2.5 inches (2.5 to 6.4 cm)
Color: Yellowish white with brown coating
Habitat: Attached to rocks in shallow water
Range: North Carolina to Texas

ZEBRA ARK *(ARCA ZEBRA)*

The zebra ark has brown-and-white stripes that resemble those of a zebra. It is sometimes called the turkey wing ark because its shape and stripes look like the wings of a wild turkey. The sturdy shell is long and narrow. Its ribs are slightly raised, smooth, and of irregular size. The zebra ark attaches itself to coral rocks or other hard surfaces. It gets washed ashore after strong waves dislodge it.

HOW TO SPOT

Size: 3 to 4 inches (7.6 to 10.2 cm)
Color: Yellowish white with reddish-brown or brown bands
Habitat: Attached to rocks in shallow water
Range: North Carolina to Florida

ATLANTIC JACKKNIFE CLAM

(ENSIS LEEI)

The Atlantic jackknife clam is also known as a razor clam. It resembles a straight razor and has sharp edges. It is long and narrow with a slight curve. The shells are thin and delicate. Jackknife clams tend to blend in with mud or sand. They live near the shoreline in the Atlantic Ocean of eastern Canada and the United States. Jackknife clams have a strong foot and are known for their ability to burrow quickly and deeply.

HOW TO SPOT

Size: 4 to 8 inches (10.2 to 20.3 cm)
Color: Black, brown, gray, yellowish, or white
Habitat: In sand or mud of shallow water
Range: Labrador, Canada, to South Carolina

WHAT ARE CLAMS?

Clams are bivalves. They have two separate equal shells, known as valves. There are two categories: hard-shelled and soft-shelled. Most clams are egg- or heart-shaped. Lesser known clams are long and tubular. They all have a muscular "foot" to dig and hide in sand or mud. Clams vary in size.

COQUINA CLAM *(DONAX VARIABILIS)*

Variable coquina is another name for this clam. The shells are small and wedge-shaped. Concentric lines mark the shells from its hinge to outer edges. Slight grooves run across the curved lines. The colors are vibrant and sometimes mixed with darker tones, inside and out. Some have rays that fan out from the hinge.

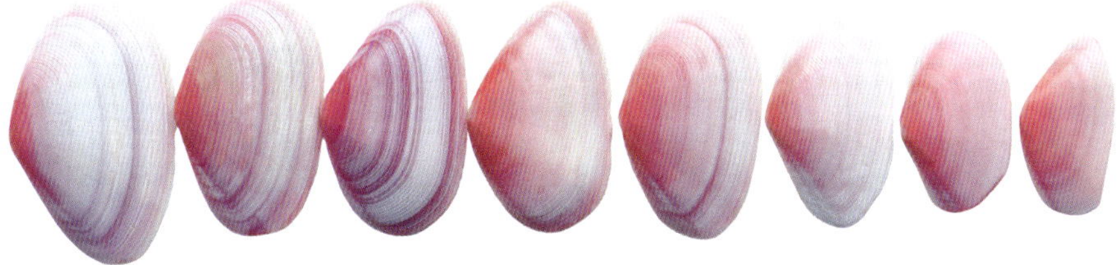

HOW TO SPOT

Size: 0.8 inches (2 cm)
Color: White with yellow, red, blue, or purple
Habitat: In sand of shallow water
Range: New York to the Gulf of Mexico

HARD-SHELLED CLAM

(MERCENARIA MERCENARIA)

The hard-shelled clam is also called a northern quahog, pronounced "koe-hog." The shells are heavy and thick. Curved growth lines are raised, but the shells have a smooth spot near the center. The egg-shaped shells are similar to many other species of clams. Although the outside of the clam is not colorful, the interior is white with purple stains. The hard-shelled clam is common on the eastern seaboard of Canada and the United States. It is a popular seafood.

HOW TO SPOT

Size: 3 to 5 inches (7.6 to 12.7 cm)
Color: White to gray
Habitat: In sand or mud
Range: Nova Scotia, Canada, to Florida

MANILA CLAM

(VENERUPIS PHILIPPINARUM)

This clam is also called a Japanese littleneck because of its origin in Japan. The shells are thick and oval. Curved growth ribs form half circles rounding from the hinge to the outer edges. Straight, narrow lines run across them. Its exterior is usually streaked with color. The inside of the shells are often tinted yellow or purple. The manila clam lives along the western coast from Canada to Mexico. It is widely eaten.

HOW TO SPOT

Size: Up to 3 inches (7.6 cm)
Color: Cream to gray, with green or brown tones
Habitat: In sand or mud
Range: British Columbia, Canada, to Baja California peninsula, Mexico

ATLANTIC STRAWBERRY COCKLE *(AMERICARDIA MEDIA)*

The Atlantic strawberry cockle has a thick, puffed out, squarish, strong shell. About 33 to 36 ribs fan out from the hinge. Low-lying curved scales are present on the ridges. The most notable feature is its reddish striping. It appears in patches across the ribs. Its curved inside edges are marked with notches. The Atlantic strawberry cockle is rarely found on beaches.

HOW TO SPOT

Size: 1 to 2 inches (2.5 to 5.1 cm)
Color: White with orange to reddish-brown marks
Habitat: In sand or mud
Range: North Carolina to Florida

WHAT ARE COCKLES?

Cockles are bivalves with rounded shells. They appear heart-shaped when turned sideways. The two halves, or valves, of the shell are equal. Evenly spaced ribs are often spiny, but they are smooth in some species. There are about 200 living species around the world. Cockles are edible, and many are used as a food source.

FLORIDA PRICKLY COCKLE

(TRACHYCARDIUM EGMONTIANUM)

The Florida prickly cockle gets its name for the short, scoop-shaped protrusions from its ribs. Their prickles, or scales, provide some protection from predators. The thick shell is circular to oval. There are deep grooves between the ridges. The rough surface has 27 to 31 ribs that extend from the hinge to the curved edges. Random spots of color mark the exterior. Pinks and purples color the glossy interior.

HOW TO SPOT

Size: 1 to 2 inches (2.5 to 5.1 cm)

Color: White to tan with yellow, brown, or purple marks

Habitat: In sand or mud

Range: North Carolina to Texas

GIANT ATLANTIC COCKLE

(DINOCARDIUM ROBUSTUM)

The giant Atlantic cockle shell is sturdy, heavy, and oval. Its valves are equal in size and shape. A unique feature is the 32 to 36 broad ribs on the inside as well as the outside. The flattened ribs on most of the shell are smooth. But the new growth of the outer edges forms rounded ridges that are scalelike. Its light colored exterior has scattered brownish spots, and the interior is pinkish.

HOW TO SPOT

Size: 2.3 to 5.3 inches (5.8 to 13.5 cm)

Color: Cream with reddish-brown spots

Habitat: In sand

Range: North Carolina to Texas

FUN FACT

Cockles have the ability to leap from their predators.

YELLOW PRICKLY COCKLE

(DALLOCARDIA MURICATA)

The yellow prickly cockle shell is slightly taller than wide. Its shape is nearly circular. It has 30 to 40 spiny ribs. The abundance of scales are somewhat beady, rather than the scoop-shaped ones on the Florida prickly cockle. Patches of color dot the exterior. Yellow or purple often streaks the interior. The yellow prickly cockle is common along the Atlantic coast of the southeast to southern United States.

HOW TO SPOT

Size: 1.5 to 2 inches (3.8 to 5.1 cm)
Color: Cream to yellowish with brownish-red marks
Habitat: In sand or mud
Range: North Carolina to Texas

BLUE MUSSEL *(MYTILUS EDULIS)*

The blue mussel shell is thin and shaped roughly like a teardrop. Concentric lines curve from the narrow end to the outer edges. The shells are dark colored and smooth. They sometimes have a skin-like brown coating and radial bands of color. The animal attaches to rocks or other hard surfaces. They can be found on both coasts of North America. Blue mussels are a popular food source around the world.

HOW TO SPOT

Size: 1.5 to 4 inches (3.8 to 10.2 cm)

Color: Dark blue to black, or purplish brown

Habitat: On intertidal rocks and hard surfaces

Range: Newfoundland, Canada, to North Carolina, and Alaska to Baja California peninsula, Mexico

WHAT ARE MUSSELS AND JINGLE SHELLS?

Mussels and jingle shells are bivalves. Jingle shells are thin, and mussel shells range from thin to moderately thick. Despite their delicate appearance, they are strong. Jingle shells tend to be more colorful but are sometimes dark like mussels. Both types of shells attach themselves to hard surfaces.

CALIFORNIA MUSSEL

(MYTILUS CALIFORNIANUS)

The California mussel is one of the largest mussels. Its elongated shells fan out in shape, and its growth lines are uneven. The arched ribs are slightly rough. The shell is thicker than the blue mussel but is often covered with the same skin-like substance. The interior has hues of gray and blue. They attach themselves to rocks or each other. The California mussel is native to North America.

HOW TO SPOT

Size: 2 to 10 inches (5.1 to 25.4 cm)
Color: Purplish gray with dark brown coating
Habitat: On rocks
Range: Alaska to central Mexico

COMMON JINGLE SHELL

(ANOMIA SIMPLEX)

The common jingle shell is thin and translucent; you can see light through it. Its shape ranges from circular to oval with uneven edges. One half of the shell is flat, and the other is convex. The flat side is more fragile. As a result, the weaker half is often broken and rarely ends up on a beach. Common jingle shells are slightly bumpy in texture.

HOW TO SPOT

Size: 1 to 3 inches (2.5 to 7.6 cm)
Color: Yellowish, orange, or silvery white
Habitat: Attached to rocks or hard surfaces
Range: Massachusetts to Florida

FUN FACT

Jingle shells got their name from the *jingle* sound produced when they clink against each other.

PRICKLY JINGLE SHELL

(HETERANOMIA SQUAMULA)

The small, thin prickly jingle shell is circular to oval. It is often irregular from the attachment it forms to a hard surface. One valve is flat with a hole near the hinge. The other is slightly convex. Each half is wrinkled in texture, one with radiating ribs and the other showing concentric growth lines. Spines are often present. Its interior is whitish and shiny.

HOW TO SPOT

Size: 0.3 to 0.8 inches (0.8 to 2 cm)
Color: White to grayish
Habitat: Attached to rocks or hard surfaces
Range: Labrador, Canada, to North Carolina

EASTERN OYSTER

(CRASSOSTREA VIRGINICA)

The eastern oyster has a thick oval-shaped shell. Irregular growth lines make most of the shell uneven or rough. Some appear to have waves of ridges. The shells are "cupped" like a scoop, but one valve is flatter than the other. Its drab color is occasionally brightened with rays in reddish hues. They are native from eastern North America to the Gulf of Mexico, spreading across a wide range. The eastern oyster is harvested for food.

HOW TO SPOT

Size: 2 to 8 inches (5.1 to 20.3 cm)

Color: Cream to grayish, sometimes with reddish-purple rays

Habitat: On hard surfaces or attached to each other

Range: New Brunswick, Canada, to Mexico

FUN FACT

Oysters form reefs by connecting together as they grow. The reefs provide a home for many other animals.

PACIFIC OYSTER *(CRASSOSTREA GIGAS)*

The Pacific oyster shell varies in shape but is generally elongated. The shells are thick and rough with ridges and grooves. Its rugged exterior along with jagged edges can make the shells sharp. It is cup-shaped like the eastern oyster, with one valve being flatter. The inside is white, sometimes with purple streaks. Because of its large size, it is also called the giant Pacific oyster.

HOW TO SPOT

Size: 2 to 10 inches (5.1 to 25.4 cm)
Color: Grayish-white, sometimes with purplish-brown spots
Habitat: Attached to rocks, soft mud, or firm sand
Range: Alaska to California

FUN FACT

The ancient Greeks crushed oyster shells to make a coarse paste for cleaning their teeth. The ingredient, calcium carbonate, is still used in some toothpastes.

WHAT ARE OYSTERS?

Oyster shells are medium to large in size. Many are irregular in shape with rugged edges. Shells are typically rough with growth ridges. Oysters cling to any solid object below water, such as rocks or piers. Most species are edible and served in some restaurants.

SAWTOOTH PEN SHELL

(ATRINA SERRATA)

The sawtooth pen shell is large and elongated. It has closely spaced small scales. They are serrated, like a saw. These shells are wedge-shaped and delicate. More than 30 ribs spread out from the long, straight hinge. The sawtooth pen shell is translucent, allowing for light to pass through it. Its interior is pearl gray to purplish.

HOW TO SPOT

Size: 6 to 12 inches (15.2 to 30.5 cm)

Color: Yellowish gray to grayish brown

Habitat: In sandy mud

Range: North Carolina to Texas

WHAT ARE PEN SHELLS?

Pen shells are bivalves with a triangular shape and a pointed end. They grow to be long and slender. The shells are typically thin and fragile. Their exterior is covered with rough, spiny ridges, and inside reveals a shiny layer near the tapered end. The sea creature buries the narrow, pointed end of its shell into sand or mud.

STIFF PEN SHELL *(ATRINA RIGIDA)*

The stiff pen shell has 15 to 25 rows of tubular scales. Its fan shape is similar to the sawtooth pen shell. But it is moderately thick-shelled and fairly strong. The sea creature burrows into their soft bottom habitat, leaving the wide edges exposed to water. Stiff pen shells are almost translucent. The interior is multicolored with hues of orange. Their exterior is often partially covered in sea growth, such as algae and sponge animals.

HOW TO SPOT

Size: 5 to 11 inches (12.7 to 27.9 cm)
Color: Dark grayish to olive brown
Habitat: In sandy mud
Range: North Carolina to Texas

FUN FACT
Black pearls are sometimes found in pen shells. They are used to make jewelry.

ATLANTIC SEA SCALLOP

(PLACOPECTEN MAGELLANICUS)

The Atlantic sea scallop is large and circular. Shells are smooth without the raised ribs noticeable on most other scallops. The two halves are different. One shell is flatter than the other. And one shows more color, sometimes in rays. The Atlantic sea scallop can be found from the Gulf of St. Lawrence in Canada to the lower east coast of the United States.

HOW TO SPOT

Size: 2 to 8 inches (5.1 to 20.3 cm)
Color: Cream, reddish pink, or brown
Habitat: In deep sandy or gravelly water
Range: Labrador, Canada, to North Carolina

WHAT ARE SCALLOPS?

Scallops have two saucer-shaped valves, although one is usually deeper than the other. Their name comes from the outer wavy edges that curve in a near half-circle. They have a straight-edged hinge that slightly extends beyond the body of the shell. They are typically colorful shells and often collected for art. Scallops live in all oceans worldwide and are a popular seafood.

BAY SCALLOP *(ARGOPECTEN IRRADIANS)*

Bay scallop shells are nearly circular. They are lightweight and thin. Radial ribs span out from the hinge in various colors. Fine, concentric growth lines run across the ridges. Bands of red or orange are sometimes present. Scalloped edges are visible. Young bay scallops attach themselves to blades of eelgrass. Bay scallops are a very common edible shellfish.

FUN FACT

Scallops use jet propulsion. They swim by rapidly opening and closing their valves as they take in water and shoot it out.

HOW TO SPOT

Size: Up to 4 inches (10.2 cm)
Color: White to dark gray with reddish-brown marks
Habitat: On muddy sand in eelgrass
Range: Massachusetts to Texas

GIANT PACIFIC SCALLOP

(PATINOPECTEN CAURINUS)

This giant scallop is sometimes known as the weathervane scallop. It is the largest scallop in the world. The two halves are thin and nearly circular, but they are different in appearance. One valve has about 17 rounded ribs, and the other has 24 flat ribs. One shell is white, and the other is colorful. The giant Pacific scallop is abundant in Alaska and Oregon and is collected for food.

HOW TO SPOT

Size: 4 to 11 inches (10.2 to 27.9 cm)

Color: White, reddish, or pinkish gray

Habitat: On or in sand or gravel

Range: Alaska to California

FUN FACT

All scallops have a great number of tiny eyes, unlike most bivalves. Some scallops have up to 200 eyes.

LION'S PAW *(NODIPECTEN NODOSUS)*

The lion's paw shells are somewhat flat and circular. They are moderately thick-shelled and heavy with broad, rounded ribs. They sometimes have bumps and rough growth ridges. These shells are colorful inside and out with hues of red. The interior shows a dark brownish red and fine tooth marks along the curved edges. It is very rare for a whole, two-valved shell to be found on a sandy beach.

HOW TO SPOT

Size: 2.5 to 6 inches (6.4 to 15.2 cm)

Color: Orange to purplish red, often with yellowish bands

Habitat: On coarse sand or debris in deep water

Range: North Carolina to Texas

FLAT ABALONE *(HALIOTIS WALALLENSIS)*

The flat abalone shell is oval and very flat. It has fine thread-like lines. There are four to eight open holes that release water. The flat abalone is a multicolored shell with an iridescent interior of pale pink and light green. The flat abalone is rare in some of its habitat range.

HOW TO SPOT

Size: 1 to 6.9 inches (2.5 to 17.5 cm)
Color: Dark red with greenish blue and white
Habitat: On or under rocks
Range: British Columbia, Canada, to California

GREEN ABALONE *(HALIOTIS FULGENS)*

The green abalone shell is shallow and oval. It is a strong, thick shell. It has irregular grooves that spiral to the outer edge. Ridges cross these grooves. There are five to seven open holes on the outer curved edge of the shell. The interior of the shell shines with bluish-green hues. The green abalone finds protection among rocks or in rock crevices.

HOW TO SPOT

Size: 6 to 8 inches (15.2 to 20.3 cm)

Color: Greenish to reddish brown

Habitat: On or among rocks in deep water

Range: California to Baja California peninsula, Mexico

WHAT ARE ABALONES?

Abalones are sea snail univalves and belong to the scientific class Gastropoda. They have a single rounded to oval-shaped shell, like a shallow bowl. A row of holes runs along one edge, numbering 8 to 38. The inside of the shell has a hard and colorful layer called nacre that makes it shine. There are about 100 species in the abalone family worldwide. Abalones are edible.

PINK ABALONE *(HALIOTIS CORRUGATA)*

The pink abalone is oval to circular with a cup shape. Its shell has spirals. The spirals are crossed by wavy ridges that give it a wrinkled texture. The shell is rough and thick with scalloped edges. Two to four raised holes appear on the outer edge above a row of knobs that circle the shell. The interior is a pearly pink with green.

HOW TO SPOT

Size: 6 to 10 inches (15.2 to 25.4 cm)
Color: Greenish to pinkish brown
Habitat: On rocks
Range: California to Baja California peninsula, Mexico

RED ABALONE *(HALIOTIS RUFESCENS)*

The red abalone has several broad, wave-like ridges that give it a lumpy appearance. Fine lines run across the protruding bands. It has three to four slightly raised oval holes near the outer edge. The interior colors range from pinkish to pale blue or green. The red abalone is the largest species of its family. Shell collectors value its unique red color, and restaurants serve the snail as a delicacy.

HOW TO SPOT

Size: 8 to 12 inches (20.3 to 30.5 cm)

Color: Brick red

Habitat: On rocks

Range: Oregon to Baja California peninsula, Mexico

EASTERN AUGER

(NEOTEREBRA DISLOCATA)

The eastern auger has a pointed top and a small opening at the larger end. The body whorls are adorned with vertical ridges. About 25 ribs mark each tier. The tiers are divided by a smaller band, and an angular groove defines each row. Eastern augers live near the water's edge along the Atlantic Ocean.

HOW TO SPOT

Size: Up to 2.5 inches (6.4 cm)
Color: Cream to tan
Habitat: In sand in shallow water
Range: Maryland to Florida

SHINY AUGER *(HASTULA HASTATA)*

The shiny auger shell has nine whorls, or tiered spirals. The shell is smooth and glossy. Closely lined vertical ribs mark each tier. Its pale color is highlighted with an orange hue. The narrow opening has a thin outer lip, and the base has a thin spiral groove. The shiny auger lives near the shoreline like the eastern auger but lives farther south in a smaller range.

HOW TO SPOT

Size: 1 to 2 inches (2.5 to 5.1 cm)
Color: White with orangish-brown bands
Habitat: In sand or mud
Range: Florida

WHAT ARE AUGERS?

Augers are long, slender shells that grow in ringed tiers. They get their name because they resemble drill bits. But they are more cone-shaped, being larger at one end and pointed at the other. Most augers inject a toxic substance known as venom into their prey. There are approximately 20 known species in North American waters.

BROWN-LINED PAPER BUBBLE

(HYDATINA VESICARIA)

The brown-lined paper bubble shell is oval and resembles a small egg. The thin shell has a flattened spire and a large, curved opening with a thin outer lip. Many spiral wavy lines mark its exterior. It sometimes shows brown spots or narrow vertical bands. The shell is smooth and glossy. The brown-lined paper bubble is found in a small area of North America.

HOW TO SPOT

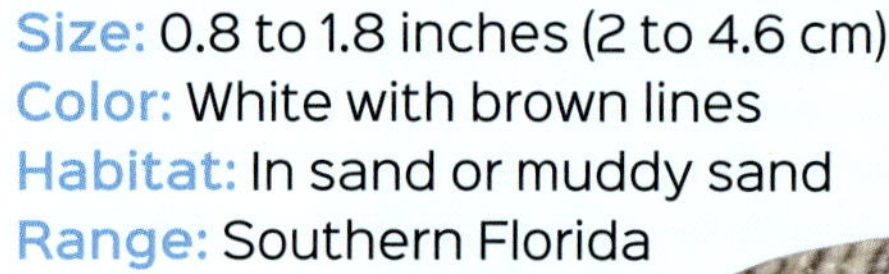

Size: 0.8 to 1.8 inches (2 to 4.6 cm)
Color: White with brown lines
Habitat: In sand or muddy sand
Range: Southern Florida

WHAT ARE BUBBLE SHELLS?

Bubble shells are oblong and globular. They look puffed out like a bubble. The shells are smooth and range from thin to thick. Bubble shells can be found in cold to tropical waters in every ocean.

CALIFORNIA BUBBLE

(BULLA GOULDIANA)

The California bubble shell is rounded, smooth, and thin. Its outline is oval-shaped. The shell is distinct with angular dark streaks or spots bordered by white. It is often coated with a thin brown skin. The California bubble shell has a long, wide opening that is round at one end. This species is the largest in the family of bubble shells.

HOW TO SPOT

Size: 1.5 to 2.5 inches (3.8 to 6.4 cm)

Color: Grayish with brown marks

Habitat: In mud or among eelgrass

Range: Alaska to Baja California, Mexico

MINIATURE MELO

(MICROMELO UNDATUS)

The miniature melo is roundish and small. It has a flattened top with a large body whorl. Its small point sinks in as the shell grows. Three red lines ring the outside and inside. Vertical wavy lines run between them and are also noticeable on the inside. The snail is also distinct with an irregular-shaped blue body and white spots. The miniature melo is a rare species.

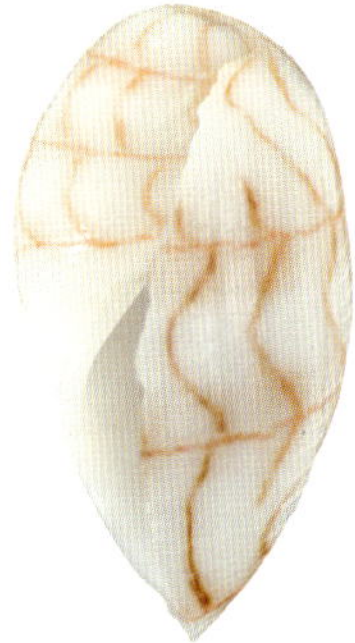

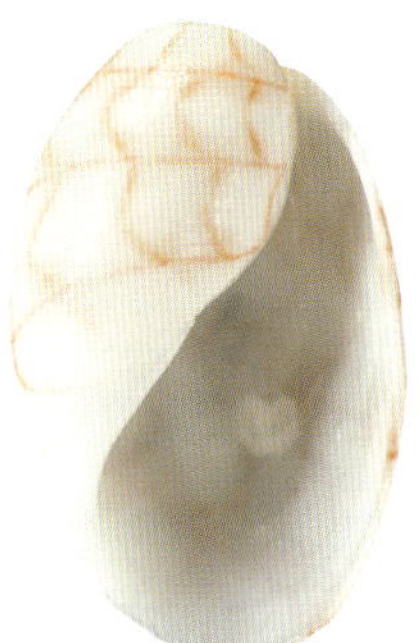

HOW TO SPOT

Size: 0.5 inches (1.3 cm)
Color: Cream with red to brown lines
Habitat: On algae in shallow water
Range: Florida and Hawaii

SOLITARY GLASSY BUBBLE

(HAMINOEA SOLITARIA)

The solitary glassy bubble is thin-shelled and oval. It is almost see-through. This small shell shows spiral grooves on a light background. It is sometimes completely white and sometimes a shade of orange speckled with white. Its opening is long with a slightly thick, white inner lip that curls in. The solitary glassy bubble shell is common along the Atlantic Ocean of North America.

HOW TO SPOT

Size: 0.3 inches (0.8 cm)
Color: Whitish to yellowish orange
Habitat: In sandy mud of shallow water
Range: Newfoundland, Canada, to Florida

DARK CERITH *(CERITHIUM ATRATUM)*

The dark cerith is also known as the Florida cerith. This slender pointed shell has many whorls. There are several beaded cords, or strings, that circle the shell. Its opening is oval-shaped. The dark cerith lives in protected areas of water such as bays and lagoons or on coral reef rock.

HOW TO SPOT

Size: 1 to 2 inches (2.5 to 5.1 cm)
Color: Whitish with reddish-brown spots
Habitat: On sand or rocks in shallow water
Range: North Carolina to Texas

IVORY CERITH *(CERITHIUM EBURNEUM)*

The ivory cerith shell has many rows of beaded spirals on its elongated shape. Ridges run vertically. It has a pointy top and an oval opening on the other end. Its outer lip is jagged and curls outward. Its curved canal protrudes from the end of the shell's opening. The ivory cerith has patches or spots of color. It is found in a small range of North America.

HOW TO SPOT

Size: 0.8 to 1.7 inches (2 to 4.3 cm)
Color: Pale cream with reddish-brown marks
Habitat: Among seagrass
Range: Florida

WHAT ARE CERITHS?

Ceriths are univalves that vary in size and decoration. They range from small to medium, and their defined rings are adorned with beads or knobs. The color varies from light to dark with spots. Ceriths look similar to augers with tiers and a pointed end. Many whorls spiral from top to bottom. Ceriths live in warm water on both coasts of North America.

LADDER HORN SNAIL

(CERITHIDEOPSIS SCALARIFORMIS)

The ladder horn snail shell is named for its ribbed-lined whorls. The numerous coarse ribs point from end to end. They sometimes have a knobby texture. Each whorl is divided by a whitish cord. Its body is a blend of colors and the tip of the shell is cream-colored. Its opening is round, brown, and with a flared, mostly white lip. Spirals mark the base of the shell. The ladder horn snail lives in warm and tropical waters.

HOW TO SPOT

Size: 0.8 to 1.5 inches (2 to 3.8 cm)
Color: Reddish brown with whitish cords and bands
Habitat: On mud flats
Range: Georgia and Florida

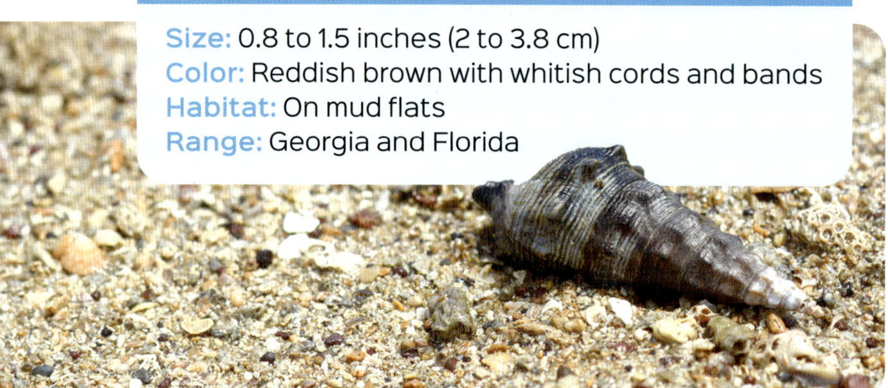

STOCKY CERITH

(CERITHIUM LITTERATUM)

The stocky cerith shell is short and wide. It has a pointed spire and straight-sided whorls. Uneven spiral cords appear knobby. There is a flattened area near the wider end. The stocky cerith has an oval opening with an outer wavy lip. Its shell is decorated with rows of dark spots inside and out. The stocky cerith is common along the southern coast of the United States.

HOW TO SPOT

Size: 0.8 to 1.5 inches (2 to 3.8 cm)

Color: Whitish with reddish-brown or black spots

Habitat: On rocks or among oyster reefs in shallow water

Range: Florida to Texas

CROWN CONCH *(MELONGENA CORONA)*

The crown conch is also called the Florida crown conch. This shell is small to medium-sized and elongated. Its whorls curve out and form tiers. It is mostly cone-shaped with a shelf-like shoulder. Pointed edges line the top whorls, giving it a crown-like appearance. The shoulder spines are triangular and hollow. It has a wide smooth opening, and its inner lip slightly twists as it curls in.

HOW TO SPOT

Size: 1 to 8 inches (2.5 to 20.3 cm)
Color: Whitish with dark brown bands
Habitat: On mud or muddy sand in shallow water
Range: Florida and Alabama

WHAT ARE CONCHS?

Conchs are usually moderate to large in size with thick, heavy shells. Their shape is unique. They have a wide body with a spiraled pointed top. A long opening stretches wide to a flared lip that shows pink to orange coloring. Many species of conchs are edible.

FLORIDA FIGHTING CONCH

(STROMBUS ALATUS)

The Florida fighting conch has a medium-sized, thick shell. Short, somewhat spiky knobs are present on the top bands. Spirals lead to a point. The texture of the body is generally smooth. This conch comes in a blend of colors, sometimes with patterns. Its interior is purplish brown to orange. The Florida fighting conch is common throughout the waters surrounding Florida and is often washed ashore on the Gulf of Mexico coast after storms.

HOW TO SPOT

Size: 3 to 4 inches (7.6 to 10.2 cm)
Color: Cream with orange, or reddish brown to dark brown
Habitat: In sandy mud
Range: North Carolina to Mexico

FUN FACT

Conch shells have been used as musical instruments for thousands of years. They are sometimes modified to be blown like a trumpet.

HORSE CONCH

(TRIPLOFUSUS GIGANTEUS)

The horse conch shell is huge. It can grow as large as 2 feet (0.6 m). This conch is the largest living sea snail in North America. The shell is thick and heavy. Ridged whorls, some with knobs, spiral to a point. Grooves between the spirals and the ribs are evident. Its light colored shell is sometimes coated with a brown, flaky skin. The inside of the shell is orange. The horse conch is a common shell in the shallow waters of the Atlantic Ocean to the Gulf of Mexico.

HOW TO SPOT

Size: Up to 2 feet (0.6 m)
Color: Cream to orange
Habitat: On sand or muddy sand in shallow water
Range: North Carolina to Mexico

FUN FACT

The horse conch uses its large, strong orange foot to kill its prey.

PINK CONCH *(ALIGER GIGAS)*

The pink conch is also known as the queen conch. It forms a large, heavy shell and can grow up to 12 inches (30.5 cm) and weigh up to 5 pounds (2.3 kg). It is whorl-shaped with short to long spines, or knobs. The exterior blends in with sand, but the interior is pink to orange. Its flared, wide, and wavy lip stretches from one end of the shell almost to its point. The pink conch is a desirable, edible snail.

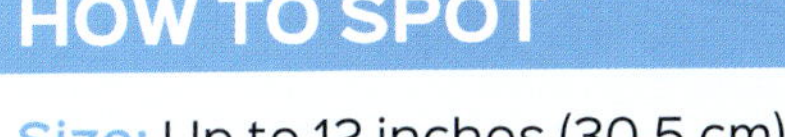

HOW TO SPOT

Size: Up to 12 inches (30.5 cm)
Color: Cream with brownish marks
Habitat: On seagrass or sand in shallow water
Range: Florida to Mexico

ALPHABET CONE *(CONUS SPURIUS)*

The alphabet cone has a mostly smooth shell with a spiraled pointy end. Thin spiral ridges form near the base. The opening is curved and narrow. Its whitish color is decorated entirely with spots. The alphabet cone is found in subtropical to tropical warm waters.

HOW TO SPOT

Size: 2 to 3 inches (5.1 to 7.6 cm)
Color: White with orange to reddish-brown spots
Habitat: In sand
Range: Florida to Mexico

WHAT ARE CONE SHELLS?

Cone shells protect highly venomous snails. They have a harpoon-shaped tooth for biting their prey. The cylindrical shell shape gives it its name. Some have a pointed end, and others are nearly flattened. They are typically colorful and patterned. Cone shells are found in oceans worldwide, usually in warm tropical waters.

CROWN CONE *(CONUS REGIUS)*

The crown cone shell has a moderately high spire with streaks of color. The rest of the shell has blotches or bands of brown shades. Its spire whorl has knobs, especially notable on the shoulder, or widest part of the shell, that give the appearance of a crown. The body spirals are separated by grooves. Its opening is long, narrow, and whitish, sometimes with brown marks along the outer lip. The crown cone can be found on the beaches of southern Florida to its islands.

HOW TO SPOT

Size: 1.5 to 3 inches (3.8 to 7.6 cm)
Color: Whitish with yellowish-brown or reddish-brown marks
Habitat: Under or on rocks in shallow water
Range: South Florida to Florida Keys

JASPER CONE *(CONUS JASPIDEA)*

The jasper cone shell is small with body whorls leading to a high spire. The spiraled end extending to a point is more elongated compared to other cone shells. It makes up about one-third of the shell length. Beaded cords are sometimes present. The body whorls are defined with grooves and marked with fine vertical ribs. Its outer lip edge is wavy. The jasper cone has blotches or streaks of color.

HOW TO SPOT

Size: Up to 1 inch (2.5 cm)
Color: Whitish with yellowish-brown or reddish-brown spots
Habitat: In sand
Range: Florida to Mexico

MAZE CONE *(CONASPRELLA MAZEI)*

The maze cone is elongated and slender with a high spire. The shell is either smooth or etched with fine-grooved spiral lines. Squarish markings dot the shell in rows that angle toward its open end. Shells of this species are very consistent in appearance throughout their range. The maze cone lives in deep waters of the Gulf of Mexico. It is a rare species.

HOW TO SPOT

Size: 1.5 to 2.5 inches (3.8 to 6.4 cm)
Color: Whitish with yellow to brown marks
Habitat: In sand of deep water
Range: Florida and in the Gulf of Mexico

FUN FACT

A valuable, rare cone shell, *Conus gloriamaris*, also called "glory of the sea," is the only known shell stolen from a museum.

ATLANTIC DEER COWRIE

(MACROCYPRAEA CERVUS)

The Atlantic deer cowrie shell is one of the largest in the cowrie family. It is elongated in shape. It can grow to larger than 7 inches (17.8 cm). The shell has many random whitish spots on a brownish background. Its appearance resembles a young deer. The opening is long and narrow, and its lips show many dark-lined teeth.

HOW TO SPOT

Size: 1.6 to 7.5 inches (4.1 to 19.1 cm)
Color: Light to dark brown with white spots
Habitat: Under rocks or coral reefs in shallow water
Range: North Carolina to Mexico

WHAT ARE COWRIES?

Cowrie shells can grow to be long and are typically cylindrical to oval. Most have a shiny glaze with colorful patterns. They have noticeable teeth lines along both edges of their shell lips. Cowries are plentiful in tropical and warm waters. There are about 200 species.

CHESTNUT COWRIE

(NEOBERNAYA SPADICEA)

The chestnut cowrie shell has an oval shape. It is slightly tear-dropped in appearance. It has a rounded body with a long, narrow opening. Many teeth line both of the shell's curled lips. The chestnut cowrie has a shiny and glossy finish. Its top side is brownish, but the sides and bottom are white. The chestnut cowrie is the only cowrie species along the Pacific Ocean coast of North America.

HOW TO SPOT

Size: 1 to 2.5 inches (2.5 to 6.4 cm)
Color: Brown and white
Habitat: In kelp beds or on rocky surfaces
Range: California to Baja California peninsula, Mexico

FUN FACT

Cowries were used as money hundreds of years ago. The strong shell and small size made them easy to carry.

FLAME HELMET *(CASSIS FLAMMEA)*

The flame helmet is roughly triangular in shape as is the large lip at the opening. Its smooth body has three whorls with rounded knobs. Ridges run toward the point of the spire. The outer smaller lip shows 11 teeth. Flame helmets have irregular fire-like splotches and streaks, which give it its common name. The flame helmet lives in tropical waters surrounding islands.

HOW TO SPOT

Size: 3 to 6 inches (7.6 to 15.2 cm)

Color: Grayish white with dark reddish brown

Habitat: In sand of shallow water

Range: Florida and Mexico

WHAT ARE HELMETS AND BONNETS?

Helmets and bonnets have medium- to large-sized shells. These heavy shells have a wide rounded body with a short spire. They resemble the shape of conch shells, but helmet shells have broader lips. This family of shells looks like helmets when resting on their flat rims. There are about 60 species living in warm waters.

KING HELMET *(CASSIS TUBEROSA)*

The king helmet is a large sea snail with a sturdy shell. Large body whorls wind around its triangular shape. Round knobs adorn three spirals at the widest part. The shell is mottled with color and marked with a crisscross pattern of fine lines. There is a large brown spot near the opening. The outer lip is marked with 11 short teeth and brownish spots, and the inner lip is partially striped with ridges. The king helmet lives in shallow southern waters.

HOW TO SPOT

Size: 4 to 11.8 inches (10.2 to 30 cm)

Color: Yellowish brown with dark brown splotches or lines

Habitat: In sand, or among seagrass beds of shallow water

Range: North Carolina to Mexico

QUEEN HELMET

(CASSIS MADAGASCARIENSIS)

The queen helmet grows to be even larger than the king helmet. It is one of the largest helmet shells. Its shape is similar to the king helmet and flame helmet. It is a heavy shell with a wide body whorl. Triangular knobs like horns appear from one outer lip around to the other at the shoulder. It has two rows of shorter knobs below. The visible inside of the lips is pale brown to salmon in color. Ten to twelve teeth are present on the outer lip.

HOW TO SPOT

Size: 4 to 14 inches (10.2 to 35.6 cm)

Color: Cream with brown marks

Habitat: On sand in shallow water

Range: North Carolina to Mexico

SCOTCH BONNET

(SEMICASSIS GRANULATA)

The Scotch bonnet is egg-shaped with a point at one end. Spiral rows are marked with colorful squares. The texture of the surface can vary. Some are smooth, and others have grooves or small bumps that create a beaded appearance. The outer lip usually shows teeth. Large quantities of the Scotch bonnet are sometimes deposited on beaches from strong winds or storms.

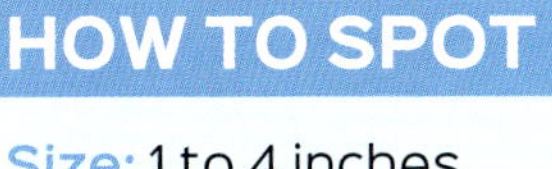

Size: 1 to 4 inches (2.5 to 10.2 cm)

Color: White to cream with orange to reddish-brown spots

Habitat: On sand in shallow water

Range: North Carolina to the Gulf of Mexico

FUN FACT

The Scotch bonnet's checkered pattern and outline slightly resemble a Scottish cap called a tam-o'-shanter. The Scottish name for a flat cap is *bonnet*.

CAYENNE KEYHOLE LIMPET

(DIODORA CAYENENSIS)

The cayenne keyhole limpet shell has an oval outline. Its cone shape is moderately high. Various sized ribs fan out from the hole to the edges. Every fourth rib is larger and more pronounced than the ones in between. The cayenne keyhole limpet is rough in texture with small knobs protruding from the ribs. It is a very common shell along the east coast of the United States.

HOW TO SPOT

Size: 0.6 to 1.8 inches (1.5 to 4.6 cm)
Color: Whitish to gray
Habitat: On and among rocks
Range: Maryland to Mexico

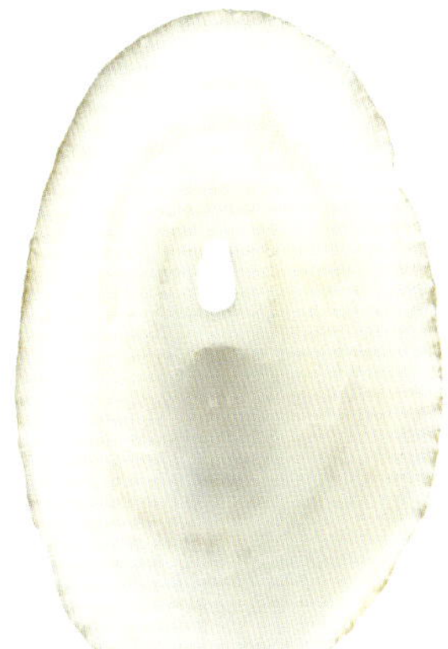

WHAT ARE LIMPETS?

Limpets have a broad conical-shaped shell that appears nearly flat. Many of them resemble a stout volcano. Some have a hole or slit, called a keyhole. They can be nearly smooth or ridged. Limpets that cling to rocks have a low shell. Those that live in calm waters have higher or narrower shells.

ROUGH KEYHOLE LIMPET

(DIODORA ASPERA)

The rough keyhole limpet has a slightly elevated cone-shaped shell. The hole at the top is off-centered. Its base forms a broad oval with somewhat scalloped edges. This shell gets its name from the coarse ribs that fan out from the hole. The ridges are crossed by growth lines. Rays of color streak the shell. The rough keyhole limpet lives throughout a long range of western North America.

HOW TO SPOT

Size: 1 to 2.8 inches (2.5 to 7.1 cm)
Color: Grayish white to yellow with purplish-gray to brown rays
Habitat: Attached to rocks
Range: Alaska to Baja California peninsula, Mexico

SHIELD LIMPET *(LOTTIA PELTA)*

The shield limpet shell is large compared to most others in the limpet family. It is heavy and moderately high. The sides are cone-shaped and slightly rounded and generally smooth. Fine ribs travel from the point to the outer edge. Wide stripes create a unique pattern. The interior is a pale color with a brown spot. The shield limpet is a West Coast shell, with the largest ones being in the north part of its range.

HOW TO SPOT

Size: 1 to 2 inches (2.5 to 5.1 cm)
Color: Grayish with white stripes
Habitat: On rocks and kelp
Range: Alaska to Baja California peninsula, Mexico

VOLCANO LIMPET

(FISSURELLA VOLCANO)

The volcano limpet has a moderately elevated cone-shaped shell. Its base and hole are oval. It has many rounded ribs, some of which are bumpy. Colorful rays streak the exterior. This pattern gives it the look of a lava-flowing volcano. Its interior keyhole is rimmed with a pink line, and the outer edge is spotted. The inside of the shell is sometimes a greenish color. The volcano limpet lives along the Pacific coast.

HOW TO SPOT

Size: 1 to 1.6 inches (2.5 to 4.1 cm)
Color: Grayish white with pink, red, or purplish rays
Habitat: On or under rocks
Range: California to Baja California peninsula, Mexico

COMMON BABY'S EAR

(SINUM PERSPECTIVUM)

The common baby's ear shell, also called the white baby ear, could be confused with the milk moon snail because of its color. However, this shell's large opening looks like an ear rather than a half-moon. The shell is oval and flattened. Its color is dull, as opposed to shiny, with visible growth lines. The common baby's ear inhabits a long range along the Atlantic coast.

HOW TO SPOT

Size: 1 to 2 inches (2.5 to 5.1 cm)
Color: White
Habitat: In sand
Range: Maryland to Texas

WHAT ARE MOON SNAILS?

Most moon snail shells are round or globular, with a large opening that looks like a half-moon. They appear to have one large whorl, which makes them distinct. The spire is short. Shells are usually smooth. There are hundreds of species found worldwide.

MILK MOON SNAIL

(POLINICES LACTEUS)

The milk moon snail is recognizable by its pure white, glossy shell. It is egg-shaped and smooth. The spire is rounded and flat, so it tends to blend in with the rest of the shell. Its underside has a deep hole next to its half-moon opening. The milk moon snail shell frequently washes up on beaches of the lower Atlantic coast of the United States.

HOW TO SPOT

Size: 0.5 to 1.5 inches (1.3 to 3.8 cm)
Color: White
Habitat: In sand
Range: North Carolina to Mexico

NORTHERN MOON SNAIL

(EUSPIRA HEROS)

The northern moon snail can grow to be a large sea snail with a large shell. It is round and smooth with a low spire. The shell is about as high as it is wide. The top whorls form a small cone. Its opening is a semicircle on its underside next to a deep small hole. The northern moon snail is very common in New England.

HOW TO SPOT

Size: 1.5 to 5 inches (3.8 to 12.7 cm)
Color: Tan to brownish gray
Habitat: In sand
Range: Labrador, Canada, to North Carolina

SHARK EYE *(NEVERITA DUPLICATA)*

The shark eye shell is mostly rounded with whorls. But its shell can be slightly flattened, giving it an oval-looking shape, and making it wider than it is high. The top small circle is often dark blue and resembles an eye. The shark eye shell is sometimes striped with color with a large brown spot on the underside. Its opening is semicircular.

HOW TO SPOT

Size: 1 to 3 inches (2.5 to 7.6 cm)
Color: Bluish to brownish gray
Habitat: In sand of shallow water
Range: Massachusetts to Texas

FUN FACT

Moon snails are predators, and their favorite food is clams. They use a sharp tooth to drill a hole into clam shells.

BLACK MUREX *(MURICANTHUS NIGRITUS)*

The black murex has a sturdy shell with six whorls and a pointed spire. Open-ended spines stand out on the entire shell. Another notable feature is the black stripes and black spines. Its opening is oval-shaped and white-rimmed, but the interior is brown. The black murex lives in warm water of the Gulf of California.

HOW TO SPOT

Size: 3 to 7.9 inches (7.6 to 20.1 cm)
Color: White and black
Habitat: On sand and gravel
Range: Baja California peninsula, Mexico, to mainland Mexico

WHAT ARE MUREXES?

Murex shells have extreme variations in size, shape, and texture. Some are decorated with long spines, some have rugged ribs, and others are smooth. They have an elongated shape with a pointed end and an oval opening. Murexes are a large family of more than 700 species worldwide.

GIANT EASTERN MUREX

(HEXAPLEX FULVESCENS)

The giant eastern murex has a large shell with a broad, cone-shaped spire. Defined body whorls are large and wavy. Vertical ribs are adorned with hollow spikes, or spines, that cover the shell. Even the lip of its opening is trimmed with spines. Fine teeth mark the outer lip of the white opening. Its interior is brown. The giant eastern murex is often found in the shallow water of northern Florida and Texas.

HOW TO SPOT

Size: 5 to 7 inches (12.7 to 17.8 cm)

Color: White to gray with reddish-brown lines

Habitat: On sand in shallow to deep water

Range: North Carolina to Texas

LACE MUREX *(CHICOREUS DILECTUS)*

The lace murex shell has an elongated shape but is relatively small in size compared to other murexes. It has a sculptural appearance with a high conical spire and remarkable protrusions. Three major ridges are decorated with long, scaly spines. Spines along one side of the opening have leaf-like edges. Short knobs appear between the ridges. The lace murex can be found throughout a large range.

HOW TO SPOT

Size: 1 to 3.3 inches (2.5 to 8.4 cm)
Color: Whitish to brown or brownish black
Habitat: On coral rubble, rocky, or sandy bottoms
Range: North Carolina to Mexico

PINK-MOUTH MUREX

(HEXAPLEX ERYTHROSTOMUS)

The pink-mouth murex shell is globular in shape with blunt spines. It is a sturdy, heavy, rugged shell. Wavy lines connect the spines that cover most of the shell. One lip flares wide and smooth, and the other is adorned with spines. The opening is circular and, as its name indicates, a noticeable bright pink spreads from inside and across its flared lips. Ridges are noticeable on its glossy interior.

HOW TO SPOT

Size: Up to 4 inches (10.2 cm)
Color: White or grayish with pink
Habitat: In sand or mud
Range: Baja California peninsula, Mexico, to mainland Mexico

LETTERED OLIVE *(OLIVA SAYANA)*

The lettered olive shell is smooth and glossy. Its elongated shape starts with a small, pointed, conical spire. Brownish speckles dot the top. Zigzag lines are characteristic of the body whorl, and the markings sometimes resemble letters. Its narrow opening widens at the base. Slanted ridges mark the lowest part of the curved edge. This species is plentiful in a large range.

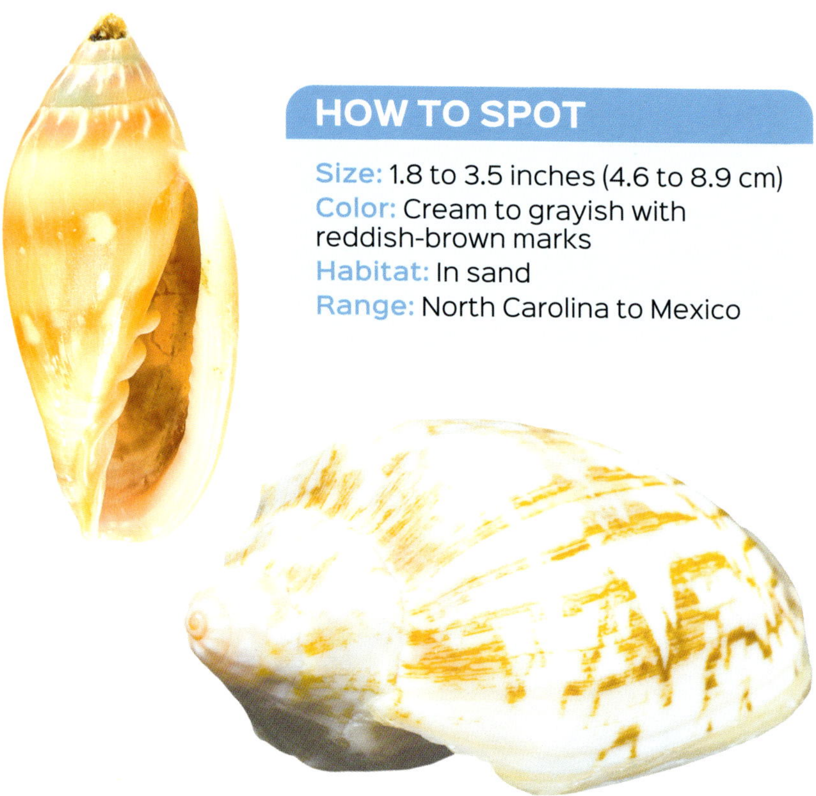

HOW TO SPOT

Size: 1.8 to 3.5 inches (4.6 to 8.9 cm)
Color: Cream to grayish with reddish-brown marks
Habitat: In sand
Range: North Carolina to Mexico

WHAT ARE OLIVE SHELLS?

Olive shells are oval and cylindrical and come in sizes similar to olives. Most have a large body whorl with a small spire. Their opening is long and narrow. Olive shells reside in tropical and temperate waters.

NETTED OLIVE *(OLIVA RETICULARIS)*

The netted olive shell is heavy and oval-shaped. It has a short, pointed spire. The spire is conical and has four whorls separated by grooves. The body consists of a long smooth whorl. The opening is long, extending the length of the body, and the outer lip is thick. Ridges, or folds, are noticeable on its lower curved opening. A netted pattern is occasionally marked with brown bands. The netted olive lives in the Gulf of Mexico.

HOW TO SPOT

Size: 1.1 to 2.3 inches (2.8 to 5.8 cm)
Color: Cream with light to reddish-brown marks
Habitat: In sand of shallow water
Range: Florida to Mexico

PURPLE DWARF OLIVE

(OLIVELLA BIPLICATA)

The purple dwarf olive shell is widely rounded compared to others in the family. Grooved brown lines divide the whorls of the spire. Its opening is shaped like an extended triangle with a thin outer lip in a purple hue. The glossy shell's color varies a bit. Sometimes it is solid, and sometimes it is striped. The purple dwarf olive is known along the western coast of North America.

HOW TO SPOT

Size: 0.5 to 1.5 inches (1.3 to 3.8 cm)
Color: Purplish to blue gray, or tan with purple stripes
Habitat: In sand of open shorelines or in water
Range: Alaska and Canada to Baja California peninsula, Mexico

VARIABLE DWARF OLIVE

(OLIVELLA MUTICA)

The variable dwarf olive shell is oval and smooth with a pointed spire. The small shell has a narrow triangular opening that is often brown. The shell's exterior color varies. Some have multiple hues or bands of color, and some are mainly one color. The variable dwarf olive lives along the eastern seaboard and on both sides of Florida.

HOW TO SPOT

Size: Up to 0.6 inches (1.5 cm)
Color: Cream with pinkish-gray or brown bands, or solid cream to brown
Habitat: In sand or shallow water
Range: New Jersey to Florida Keys

BEADED PERIWINKLE

(CENCHRITIS MURICATUS)

The beaded periwinkle shell is covered in tiny beads that vary in size. The adorned ridges spiral in rows from the point to the opening on the underside. Its interior is brown. The shell rests at a slant. It survives on rocks in zones that have splashes or sprays of water to keep it moist. The beaded periwinkle is common in the Florida Keys.

HOW TO SPOT

Size: Up to 1.2 inches (3 cm)
Color: Yellowish gray or bluish gray with white knobs
Habitat: On rocks
Range: Southern Florida to the Florida Keys

CHECKERED PERIWINKLE

(LITTORINA SCUTULATA)

The checkered periwinkle shell has characteristic white checkers on a dark background. However, the pattern is occasionally absent. Sometimes the shell is pale in color with a band of dark brown. Its shape is roughly round and elongated with a sharp point. It has a smooth surface. The checkered periwinkle shell displays a purplish interior.

HOW TO SPOT

Size: Up to 0.6 inches (1.5 cm)
Color: Brown to black-purple with white spots, or cream with brownish bands
Habitat: On rocky shorelines
Range: Alaska to Oregon

WHAT ARE PERIWINKLES?

Periwinkles are small- to medium-sized shells. Some are smooth and others are sculpted with ridges and knobs. They are typically thick and somewhat round. Many survive in wide cracks of rocks or hide in seaweed. Some live above water most of the time on rocks or seagrasses. Periwinkles have a wide range from cold to tropical waters.

COMMON PERIWINKLE

(LITTORINA LITTOREA)

The common periwinkle shell is roughly egg-shaped with a pointed end and resembles a turban shell. Its thick shell has six to seven whorls with some fine lines. It is typically light in color with spirals of darker shades. It has a white base near the circular opening, and its interior is dark brown. The common periwinkle is edible but rarely eaten in North America.

HOW TO SPOT

Size: 0.6 to 1.5 inches (1.5 to 3.8 cm)
Color: Grayish to gray-brown with dark brown bands
Habitat: On rocks near shores
Range: Labrador, Canada, to Maryland

ZEBRA PERIWINKLE

(ECHINOLITTORINA ZICZAC)

The zebra periwinkle shell has a zigzag pattern. The streaks of color make their way from the point to the base. It is small in size and about as wide as it is long. The conical spire is narrow. It shows defined tiers of whorls with fine grooves. The shell sits at an angle. Its interior is brown. An abundance of zebra periwinkles hide in rock crevices or among rocks in warm water.

HOW TO SPOT

Size: Up to 0.9 inches (2.3 cm)
Color: Whitish to gray with brown streaks
Habitat: On rocks or in crevices near shore
Range: Florida to Mexico

CHOCOLATE-LINED TOP SHELL

(CALLIOSTOMA JAVANICUM)

The chocolate-lined top shell gets its name from the dark brown spirals that stand out on its pale-colored shell. Even the base has the chocolate colored swirls. Its base cuts in at a sharp angle. Some of the shell's whorls are decorated with tiny beads. There is a centered hollow space at the bottom that resembles a belly button. The chocolate-lined top shell is rare and can be found in various depths of the Gulf of Mexico.

HOW TO SPOT

Size: Up to 1.4 inches (3.6 cm)
Color: Cream with dark brown rings
Habitat: In sandy coral of shallow to deep water
Range: Florida Keys and in the Gulf of Mexico

WHAT ARE TOP SHELLS?

Top snails or top shells are cone-shaped with spirals. The shells resemble a spinning top toy. Their exteriors can be smooth, glossy, or sculptured with rings, ridges, and knobs. All top shells have the nacreous, pearly interior.

GRANULOSE TOP SHELL

(CALLIOSTOMA SUPRAGRANOSUM)

The granulose top shell is small and thick. Its mostly convex whorls are slightly angled with beaded threads. The shell is shiny with a unique color pattern. Its opening is round and shows a shimmering white interior. The granulose top shell is plentiful in rocky areas of the southern Pacific Ocean.

HOW TO SPOT

Size: Up to 0.5 inches (1.3 cm)

Color: Light yellowish brown with white marks

Habitat: On rocks

Range: California to Baja California peninsula, Mexico

PURPLE-RINGED TOP SHELL

(CALLIOSTOMA ANNULATUM)

The purple-ringed top shell shines with colors of gold and orange and spirals of pale purple. Its rows of cords are beaded with dots of pinkish to brownish hues. The thin shell tilts to an angle with a flattened base. Its oval opening has a thin white lip. The purple-ringed top shell is often found on kelp blades in the northern range.

HOW TO SPOT

Size: 0.6 to 1.3 inches (1.5 to 3.3 cm)

Color: Gold with purple rings

Habitat: On kelp or rocks

Range: Alaska to Baja California peninsula, Mexico

WEST INDIAN TOP SHELL

(CITTARIUM PICA)

The West Indian top shell is about as high as it is wide. This shell is heavy. It has rounded whorls separated by hidden lines. Rough slanted ribs adorn the whorls along with a dark zigzag pattern. The bottom is smooth with a funnel-shaped hole. Its opening is round and white. This shell was once found in the Florida Keys. Today, it lives in the Gulf of Mexico around the Yucatan Peninsula.

HOW TO SPOT

Size: 2 to 5.5 inches (5.1 to 14 cm)
Color: Cream with purplish-black splotches
Habitat: Among rocks of shallow water
Range: Mexico

ANGULAR TRITON

(CYMATIUM FEMORALE)

The angular triton has an uneven, roughly triangular shell shape. The spire is short compared to its body and consists of spiraled knobs. Two sharp ridges point out from each side. Wide, spiral ribs are adorned with rough knobs that get larger around the opening on the outer lip. Its shell has obvious vertical ridges that mark where the opening once was. The angular triton lives in warm water.

HOW TO SPOT

Size: 6.9 to 8.3 inches (17.5 to 21.1 cm)
Color: Pale yellow to light brownish with white knobs
Habitat: Shallow water
Range: South Florida and in the Gulf of Mexico

WHAT ARE TRITONS?

Tritons have a singular shell with a large body whorl and a pointed spire. Some shells have ridges or knobs. They resemble conchs and whelks, have a thick shell, and can grow to 20 inches (50.8 cm). Tritons often have a thick coating with long hairs.

ATLANTIC HAIRY TRITON

(MONOPLEX PILEARIS)

The medium- to large-sized Atlantic hairy triton shell spreads across a wide range of water, including the Atlantic, Pacific, and Indian Oceans. But it lives in a small area of North America. It can be found in the warm waters of Florida and the Gulf of Mexico. Its shell is elongated with a tall spire. Spiral ridges span the length with ribs running perpendicular to them. The opening is brown with white markings like teeth. The Atlantic hairy triton is protected by thick hair.

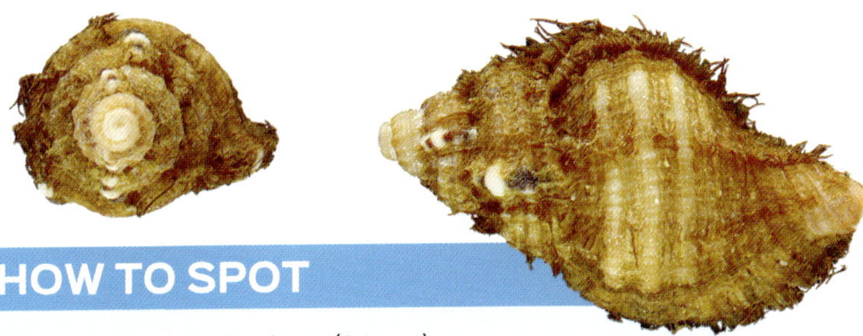

HOW TO SPOT

Size: Up to 5.5 inches (14 cm)
Color: Yellowish brown with chestnut spirals
Habitat: On coarse bottoms among reefs
Range: Florida, Hawaii, and in the Gulf of Mexico

OREGON TRITON

(FUSITRITON OREGONENSIS)

The Oregon hairy triton is another name for this shell that is bristle-coated. Spirals of bristles cover most of the shell. It is thin and lightweight. Whorls round out the shell and tiers of the spire are topped with a pointed end. There is a wide, oval opening near the other end. The lips are white with the outer lip showing ridges. Ribs protrude across the well-defined whorls. The Oregon triton originated on the northwestern coast of North America.

HOW TO SPOT

Size: 3 to 5.1 inches (7.6 to 13 cm)
Color: Cream to light brown with gray-brown bristles
Habitat: On sand and rubble from shallow to deep water
Range: Alaska to California

TRITON'S TRUMPET

(CHARONIA TRITONIS)

The triton's trumpet is a big sea snail that creates a very large shell. The shell is elongated with a spiraled point on one end and an oval opening on the other. Folds are present on both outward-curling lips. Deep grooves ring the body of the shell. A crescent pattern, sometimes splotchy, is displayed on the whorls. Streaks of orange-brown spread across its white opening. The triton's trumpet lives in the Pacific Ocean.

HOW TO SPOT

Size: Up to 24 inches (61 cm)
Color: Cream with brown marks
Habitat: Among coral reefs in moderately deep water
Range: Hawaii

FUN FACT
The triton's trumpet snail helps in preserving coral reefs. It feeds on the crown-of-thorn starfish that eats away at coral.

CHESTNUT TURBAN

(TURBO CASTANEA)

The chestnut turban shell is small in size, being almost equal in length and width. Its appearance comes in a range of colors and textures. It has a high spire with beaded spiral cords. Random colored spots dot the shell. The surface is sometimes rough with scaly knobs. Its opening is round and shiny white. The chestnut turban is a very common shell of the southeastern United States.

HOW TO SPOT

Size: 1 to 1.8 inches (2.5 to 4.6 cm)
Color: Grayish to brown or orange with white or brown spots
Habitat: Under or among rocks in shallow water
Range: North Carolina to Florida

WHAT ARE TURBAN SHELLS?

Turban shells look similar to top shells or like the headwear, a turban. They are thick shells that grow in a range of sizes and textures. Some are less than 1 inch (2.5 cm), and others are about 8 inches (20.3 cm). The shell can be smooth or sculpted.

GREEN STAR SHELL

(LITHOPOMA TUBER)

The green star shell is about as wide as it is high. The thick, heavy shell is cone-shaped with rounded whorls. The wide ribs slant across the growth lines and sometimes have knobs. Its colors create a crisscross pattern. Random spots are also present. The green star shell has an oval, pearly white opening.

HOW TO SPOT

Size: 1 to 3 inches (2.5 to 7.6 cm)
Color: Greenish to brown with white spots or lines
Habitat: Among rocks and on reefs
Range: Southeast Florida to the Florida Keys

RED TURBAN *(LITHOPOMA GIBBEROSA)*

The red turban shell has a low conical shape with a flattened spire. Sculptured spirals have slanted ribs running across them from top to bottom. Some are bumpy. The base has semicircular cords and a pearly white opening. Its exterior is often coated with a coarse brown layer. The red turban is found along the lengthy western coastline of North America.

HOW TO SPOT

Size: 1.5 to 3 inches (3.8 to 7.6 cm)
Color: Reddish or yellowish brown
Habitat: On rocks
Range: Alaska to Mexico

WAVY TURBAN *(MEGASTRAEA UNDOSA)*

The wavy turban is a broad, tilted shell. It rests at an angle over its opening. A spiral wavy cord winds its way from the point to the base. Slanted, slightly knobby ridges adorn its whorls. Spirals on the bottom curve out from its opening. The shell is covered in a tough brown substance. Underneath, there is a shiny layer.

HOW TO SPOT

Size: 2 to 6 inches (5.1 to 15.2 cm)

Color: Tan to light brown

Habitat: In rocky areas in shallow water

Range: California to Baja California peninsula, Mexico

BORING TURRET

(TURRITELLA ACROPORA)

The boring turret has many lines in a spiral pattern. Grooves are noticeable between each whorl. Each tier is slightly wider and longer than the previous one. The top is pointed, and its opening is circular. Its base is angled. Boring turrets have blotches or streaks of dark color.

HOW TO SPOT

Size: 1 to 1.6 inches (2.5 to 4.1 cm)

Color: Cream to pale yellow or brown with dark brown marks

Habitat: In sand of moderately shallow water

Range: North Carolina to Texas

EASTERN TURRITELLA

(TURRITELLA EXOLETA)

The eastern turritella shell is slender. Its small size has many tiers of growth. The ribbed whorls are concave, curving inward, unlike most turrets. Cords stand out between the whorls. It has a small square-shaped opening opposite its pointy top. Vertical, wavy lines of color decorate the shell from top to bottom. The eastern turritella is a common shell.

HOW TO SPOT

Size: 1 to 3 inches (2.5 to 7.6 cm)

Color: Cream with light brown marks

Habitat: In sandy water

Range: South Carolina to Mexico

WHAT ARE TURRETS AND WORM SHELLS?

Turret shells are shaped like a corkscrew. They have many whorls in a spiral with a pointed top and a small opening on the other end. The shells appear similar to augers, but their bodies are usually more convex, so their whorls bulge out slightly. Worm shells start out like a turret with a spiraled top but become uncoiled and take on irregular shapes.

FARGO WORM *(VERMICULARIA FARGOI)*

The Fargo worm shell is tubular and thick. Its diameter is about 0.4 inches (1 cm). The top spirals remain tightly coiled and the remainder twists open, getting slightly wider as it grows. The body whorls have strong spiral ribs. A blend of colors from pale to dark coils the exterior. The Fargo worm snail is quite common on southwest beaches of Florida.

HOW TO SPOT

Size: Up to 3 inches (7.6 cm)
Color: Cream with brown
Habitat: On mud or hard surfaces
Range: Florida to Texas

FLORIDA WORM

(VERMICULARIA KNORRII)

The Florida worm grows a shell similar to the Fargo worm. Its tightly wound spire is slightly shorter. It stretches apart from there in an irregular manner, curling or twisting like a worm. The pointy tip of the shell is white, but the remainder becomes a shade of brown. The Florida worm snail is typically found in warm waters.

Size: Up to 3 inches (7.6 cm)
Color: White to yellowish brown
Habitat: Near shoreline or coral reefs
Range: North Carolina to Mexico

DUBIOUS VOLUTE *(SCAPHELLA DUBIA)*

The dubious volute has an elongated slender shell. A rounded point leads to a tiered spire. Vertical ribs and fine spiral lines are visible on its whorls. Folds, or ripples, run the length of the shell. Rows of colored squares dot the exterior. The dubious volute is rare and found only in the Gulf of Mexico.

HOW TO SPOT

Size: 2.5 to 7.8 inches (6.4 to 19.8 cm)
Color: Cream to tan with brown squares
Habitat: In sandy water
Range: Florida to Mexico

JUNONIA *(SCAPHELLA JUNONIA)*

The junonia shell is typical of volutes with its elongated shape and long, curved opening. Its outer lip is sharp. The lower part of the inner lip flares out with four distinct folds, or ridges. The spire has slightly convex whorls, and the body is mostly smooth. Spots of color decorate the shell from end to end. Junonia shells are rarely washed up on beaches.

HOW TO SPOT

Size: 2.5 to 6.1 inches (6.4 to 15.5 cm)
Color: Cream to pinkish with brown squarish spots
Habitat: In sand of deep water
Range: Florida to Mexico

WHAT ARE VOLUTES?

Volute shells are medium to large in size. They are usually long and oval. Most are smooth, though some have ornamentation such as knobs. More than 200 species live in oceans around the world.

KNOBBED WHELK *(BUSYCON CARICA)*

The knobbed whelk is a large, thick shell with a wide orange opening. Its spire forms a broad cone with rounded knobs encircling each edge. Pointed knobs protrude from the body whorl. Its wide shape tapers near the bottom. The knobbed whelk is a common shell of the Atlantic Ocean.

HOW TO SPOT

Size: 4 to 12 inches (10.2 to 30.5 cm)
Color: Ivory to pale gray or brown
Habitat: On sand in shallow water
Range: Massachusetts to Florida

LIGHTNING WHELK

(SINISTROFULGUR SINISTRUM)

The lightning whelk shell is unique with a left-sided opening. Most shells open on the right. The shell gets its name from the jagged lines, like streaks of lightning. They give the appearance of folds or waves encircling the shell. The lightning whelk has a short, pointed spire and a large, long body. Triangular knobs adorn the shoulder of the shell. Its interior is a reddish-brown color. Spiral bands or streaks of color decorate the exterior of the shell.

HOW TO SPOT

HOW TO SPOT

Size: 7.9 to 17.7 inches (20.1 to 45 cm)

Color: White with grayish-brown bands

Habitat: In sand or mud of shallow water

Range: New Jersey to Texas

WHAT ARE WHELKS?

Whelk shells vary in shape, size, and sculpture. Most have a spacious body to accommodate large sea snails. The species is huge in number with more than 1,500 known worldwide. Whelks are found in all oceans from cold waters to the tropics.

NEW ENGLAND NEPTUNE

(NEPTUNEA LYRATA)

The New England Neptune shell is broadly shaped. Pronounced spiral ridges ring the exterior of the spire and body, becoming less noticeable near the bottom. Ribs run vertically on the whorls. Its opening is wide, and an outer wavy-edged lip is white with brown lines. The New England Neptune is also known as the wrinkled whelk.

HOW TO SPOT

Size: 3.5 inches (8.9 cm)
Color: Cream to grayish white with reddish brown
Habitat: On rocky bottoms
Range: Nova Scotia, Canada, to Massachusetts

PEAR WHELK *(FULGUROPSIS SPIRATA)*

The pear whelk is pear- or fig-shaped with a long, wide opening that tapers to a canal. The long outer lip is thin and curves outward. Its opening is reddish brown with spiral lines. A short spire is topped with a point. The body of the shell is marked with spiral ridges and vertical ribs. Its pale color is irregularly streaked or wrapped in shades of brown. This species is found in the Atlantic Ocean and the Gulf of Mexico.

HOW TO SPOT

Size: Up to 6 inches (15.2 cm)
Color: Cream with brown streaks
Habitat: On sand in shallow water
Range: North Carolina to Mexico

BLACK KATY CHITON

(KATHARINA TUNICATA)

The black katy chiton shell has a leathery texture. Most of its shell, or its girdle, is black and stretches across the bulk of the plates. But the exposed portion of the valves on top of the shell is whitish to gray. The black katy chiton lives attached to exposed rocks and withstands waves and currents. Some native groups of Canada call this chiton "sea prune."

HOW TO SPOT

Size: Up to 4.7 inches (11.9 cm)
Color: Gray with shiny black
Habitat: On rocks
Range: Alaska to California

WHAT ARE CHITONS?

Chiton shells are in the scientific class known as Polyplacophora. They are oval-shaped, single shells with symmetrical sides. The eight-pieced, overlapping valves are their most distinctive feature. The valves, or plates, are movable. There are about 1,000 species worldwide.

GIANT PACIFIC CHITON

(CRYPTOCHITON STELLERI)

The giant Pacific chiton is also known as the gumboot. Some experts think this nickname came from its resemblance to a rubber boot. It is the largest chiton in the world. Its shape is somewhat oval, flat, and lumpy. The butterfly-shaped plates are engulfed by the rest of its skin-like shell. A bumpy texture coats the entire thick shell and is unique to this species. The giant Pacific chiton's protective plates sometimes wash up on beaches.

HOW TO SPOT

Size: 5 to 13 inches (12.7 to 33 cm)
Color: Reddish brown
Habitat: Among rocks
Range: Alaska to California

FUN FACT

The giant Pacific chiton gets its color from the red algae it eats and the red algae that cling to it.

LINED CHITON *(TONICELLA LINEATA)*

The lined chiton shell is well decorated with lines, spots, and colors. Its name comes from the diagonal marks on the plates. Pale spots outline its oval shape. Various colors camouflage the sea animal. The shell's surface is smooth and shiny. The lined chiton can be found in the Pacific Northwest to southern California living among rocks or groups of purple sea urchins on the ocean floor.

HOW TO SPOT

Size: 1 to 2 inches (2.5 to 5.1 cm)
Color: Yellow, orange, red, or blue with brown lines and yellowish spots
Habitat: On or among rocks
Range: Alaska to California

MOSSY CHITON *(MOPALIA MUSCOSA)*

The mossy chiton shell has hair-like bristles on the outer ring. Its small, oval shell is drab in color, and the plates are often covered in algae or barnacles. The mossy girdle is the most distinct feature. The interior plates are blue-green. The mossy chiton lives throughout an extended range covering all three continental countries of North America.

HOW TO SPOT

Size: 1.2 to 3.9 inches (3 to 9.9 cm)
Color: Brown or gray-green with black bristles
Habitat: On rocky shores
Range: Alaska to Baja California peninsula, Mexico

GLOSSARY

camouflage
To blend or hide through color, marks, or shape.

concentric
Curved lines with the same center point.

decompose
To break down or decay.

exoskeleton
A hard, protective covering of an animal.

intertidal
Shoreline that is sometimes covered with water; the area between the high-tide mark and the low-tide mark.

iridescent
Shimmery or glossy and sometimes rainbow-like.

lagoon
Shallow water protected by a reef or peninsula.

nacre
A shiny, smooth substance inside some seashells; known as “mother of pearl.”

protrusion
Something that sticks out or juts out from a surface.

radial
Describing rays that fan out from a central point.

temperate
A consistently mild temperature.

valve
One half of a bivalve seashell. Also, the pieces, or plates, of a chiton shell.

whorl
One complete spiral or turn.

TO LEARN MORE

FURTHER READINGS

Farley, Christen. *The Little Book of Shells: A Guide to Shells and the Amazing Creatures Who Make Them*. Bushel & Peck Books, 2022.

Panlasigui, Stephanie and Zambello, Erika. *Seashells & Beachcombing for Kids*. Adventure Publications, 2023.

Scales, Helen. *What a Shell Can Tell*. Phaidon Press, 2022.

ONLINE RESOURCES

To learn more about seashells, please visit **abdobooklinks.com** or scan this QR code. These links are routinely monitored and updated to provide the most current information available.

PHOTO CREDITS

Cover Photos: Alexey Masliy/Shutterstock, front (Atlantic strawberry cockle); Daniel Wright98/Shutterstock, front (eastern auger); Ed Reschke/Photodisc/Getty Images, front (Fargo worm); Fotana/Shutterstock, front (triton's trumpet); Realto/Shutterstock, front (lion's paw); DEA/G. CIGOLINI/De Agostini/Getty Images, front (Atlantic deer cowrie); Henner Damke/Shutterstock, front (miniature melo); Slimoche/iStock/Getty Images, front (coquina clam); Jon G. Fuller/VWPics/Universal Images Group/Getty Images, front (pink-mouth murex); Mihiripix/Shutterstock, front (lightning whelk); Daniel Novak/Shutterstock, front (Florida fighting conch); Nigel Stripe/Shutterstock, front (Atlantic sea scallop); Yossi James/Shutterstock, front (ark clam); Elizabeth Fernandez/Moment/Getty Images, back (coquina clams)
Interior Photos: James St. John/Flickr, 1 (left), 1 (middle center), 23 (top), 35 (top left), 35 (top right), 38 (right); Mollusks Collection/Bailey-Matthews National Shell Museum (BMSM), 1 (top center), 8 (bottom), 9 (top), 11 (bottom), 12 (bottom), 19 (top), 21 (top), 42 (top), 44 (top), 44 (middle), 44 (bottom), 46 (top), 54 (left), 54 (right), 72 (top), 94 (bottom right), 96 (top left), 97 (bottom), 98, 112 (center), 112 (top right); Shellnut/Wikimedia Commons, 1 (bottom left), 71, 83 (top), 86, 88 (top right); 2Dvisualize/Shutterstock, 1 (top right), 80 (top); JH PETE CARMICHAEL/NHPA/Photoshot/Newscom, 1 (bottom right), 32 (bottom), 102 (top right); E. A. Lazo-Wasem/Yale Peabody Museum/Wikimedia Commons, 4 (top right), 25 (bottom), 43; H. Zell/Wikimedia Commons, 4 (bottom left), 5 (top right), 21 (bottom), 58, 61 (top), 62, 64, 65 (top), 66, 75, 85 (top), 87, 91, 94 (top left, bottom center), 95; Alexey Masliy/Shutterstock, 4 (bottom middle left), 18 (right), 18 (left), 45, 90; DEA/G. CIGOLINI/De Agostini/Getty Images, 4 (bottom middle right), 56 (left), 56 (right); Ria Tan/Flickr, 4 (bottom right), 24 (top); Bonnie Taylor Barry/Shutterstock, 5 (top left), 33 (top), 72 (bottom), 99; Anatoliy Berislavskiy/Shutterstock, 5 (top middle), 69 (bottom); Fotana/Shutterstock, 5 (bottom left), 89 (right); xiao zhou/iStock/Getty Images, 5 (bottom middle), 13 (top), 96 (bottom); 977_ReX_977/Shutterstock, 5 (bottom right), 51 (top); LarryB79/Shutterstock, 8 (top); Dinushika-photography/Shutterstock, 9 (bottom); Norma Stamp at Sunny Daze/Shutterstock, 10 (top); Erica Finstad/iStock/Getty Images, 10 (bottom); Andrew Cannizzaro/Flickr, 11 (top left); imageBROKER/Christian Hütter/Newscom, 11 (top right); Florida Fish and Wildlife Conservation Commission (FWC)/Flickr, 12 (top); George Melin/Shutterstock, 13 (bottom); Matauw/iStock/Getty Images, 14 (top); Pixelelfe/iStock/Getty Images, 14 (bottom); Elizabeth Fernandez/Moment/Getty Images, 15 (top); Slimoche/iStock/Getty Images, 15 (bottom); eastriverstudio/iStock/Getty Images, 16 (top center), 16 (bottom); Encyclopaedia Britannica/Universal Images Group/Getty Images, 16 (top right); BSIP/Universal Images Group/Getty Images, 17 (top); starry sky/Shutterstock, 17 (bottom); Nick Greaves/Shutterstock, 19 (bottom); Tim Heusinger Von Waldegge/Dreamstime.com, 20 (top); Matthew L Niemiller/Shutterstock, 20 (bottom); Arterra/Universal Images Group/Getty Images, 22 (top); Robert L. Potts / Design Pics/Getty Images, 22 (bottom); Yogevika/Dreamstime.com, 23 (bottom); Ingrid Maasik/Shutterstock, 24 (bottom); Rainer Borcherding/Wadden Sea Conservation Station/BeachExplorer, 25 (top); Dendroica cerulea/Flickr, 26 (top); Gilbert S. Grant/Shutterstock, 26 (bottom); Picture Partners/Shutterstock, 27 (right); Westend61/Getty Images, 27 (left); Janson Jones/iNaturalist, 28 (top); Matthew R McClure/Shutterstock, 28 (bottom), 31 (left), 103 (bottom); Fritzmann2002/Wikimedia Commons, 29 (top); KathyDentzKeith/Shutterstock, 29 (bottom); Nigel Stripe/Shutterstock, 30 (top); Victor1153/Shutterstock, 30 (bottom); Ethan Daniels/Shutterstock, 31 (right); LeeMarUSA/Shutterstock, 32 (top); Realto/Shutterstock, 33 (bottom); Chris Lanczycki/Department of Invertebrate Zoology/Smithsonian National Museum of Natural History, 34 (top), 112 (bottom right); steve estvanik/Shutterstock, 34 (bottom);

vickip2/Flickr, 35 (bottom); Marc Conlin/Visual&Written/Newscom, 36 (top left); Jan Delsing/BioLib, 36 (top right); LEON FELIPE CHARGOY/Shutterstock, 36 (bottom); Heather Kramp, NOAA California Sea Grant State Fellow 2017/Flickr, 37 (top left); Brent Durand/Moment/Getty Images, 37 (top right); Nonthawit Doungsodsri/Shutterstock, 37 (bottom); Daniel Wright98/Shutterstock, 38 (left); Lardeur A./Muséum national d'Histoire naturelle, Paris (France), Collection: Molluscs (IM), Specimen MNHN-IM-2013-71324/Wikimedia Commons, 39; Xiao Zhou/Dreamstime.com, 40 (top left), 77; niet van toepassing/Rijksmuseum/Wikimedia Commons, 40 (top right); Harry Rose/Flickr, 40 (bottom); Jonathan Coffin/Flickr, 41 (top); Robin Gwen Agarwal (ANudibranchMom on iNaturalist)/Flickr, 41 (bottom); Henner Damke/Shutterstock, 42 (bottom); jayjayoo7_com/iStock/Getty Images, 46 (bottom); Humberto Ramirez/Moment/Getty Images, 47 (top); Udo Schmidt/Flickr, 47 (bottom); Ach Haikal Hilmi Mustofa/Shutterstock, 48 (top); SusieQ2022/Shutterstock, 48 (bottom); ulrich missbach/Shutterstock, 49 (top); Daniel Novak/Shutterstock, 49 (bottom); Mihiripix/Shutterstock, 50 (top), 101 (top), 101 (bottom); David M. Schrader/Shutterstock, 50 (bottom); Alex James Bramwell/Shutterstock, 51 (bottom); Ed Reschke/Photodisc/Getty Images, 52 (left), 96 (top right); GYAN PRATIM RAICHOUDHURY/Shutterstock, 52 (right); Nick Zantop/Wikimedia Commons, 53 (top); manuelramalho/iNaturalist, 53 (bottom); Rabiller M. & Richard G./Muséum national d'Histoire naturelle, Paris (France), Collection: Molluscs (IM), Specimen MNHN-IM-2013-60518/Wikimedia Commons, 55, 112 (top left); Philip Garner/Shutterstock, 57 (top), 84 (top); Jon G. Fuller/VWPics/Universal Images Group/Getty Images, 57 (bottom), 73 (left), 73 (right); Marli Anders Esmeriz/Shutterstock, 59 (top), 59 (bottom); Wilfredor/Wikimedia Commons, 60 (middle); Paul Orr/Shutterstock, 61 (bottom), Smithsonian National Museum of Natural History, 63 (top); J. Maughn/Flickr, 63 (bottom); The World Traveller/iStock/Getty Images, 65 (bottom); Kazakov Maksim/Shutterstock, 67 (top); Manuel Caballer/Muséum national d'Histoire naturelle, Paris (France), Collection: Molluscs (IM), Specimen MNHN-IM-2000-5245/Wikimedia Commons, 67 (bottom); Robert Aguilar/Smithsonian Environmental Research Center/Flickr, 68 (top); 86Frankb/Shutterstock, 68 (bottom); Lost Mountain Studio/Shutterstock, 69 (top); Taweesak Sriwannawit/Shutterstock, 70, 112 (bottom left); Hectonichus/Wikimedia Commons, 71; Luis Diaz Devesa/Moment/Getty Images, 74 (left), 89 (left); Yingna Cai/Shutterstock, 74 (right); Steve Lonhart/SIMoN/MBNMS/NOAA Office of National Marine Sanctuaries/Wikimedia Commons, 76 (top left); Gustav Paulay/Florida Museum of Natural History Invertebrate Zoology/GBIF.org, 76 (top right); shari.a.images/Shutterstock, 79 (bottom); Llez/Wikimedia Commons, 78 (top); EAGiven/iStock/Getty Images, 78 (bottom); randimal/iStock/Getty Images, 79; Pan Stock/Shutterstock, 80 (bottom); Nandani Bridglal/Dreamstime.com, 81; Nestor Ardila/Wikimedia Commons, 82; Gustav Paulay/Florida Museum of Natural History/InvertEBase, 83 (bottom); Paul Starosta/Stone/Getty Images, 84 (bottom), 102 (bottom left); elena moiseeva/Shutterstock, 85 (bottom); Ed Bierman/Flickr, 88 (bottom); Miglena Pencheva/Shutterstock, 92 (top); Steven Maltby/Shutterstock, 92 (bottom); DavidKennedy/Shutterstock, 93 (top), 93 (bottom); PrashantSnapshot/Shutterstock, 94 (bottom left); JoanneStrell/Shutterstock, 97 (top); EWY Media/Shutterstock, 100 (top); bddigitalimages/Shutterstock, 100 (bottom); editha/Shutterstock, 103 (top); Gerald Corsi/iStock/Getty Images, 104 (top); Minette Layne-Worthey/Flickr, 104 (bottom); awesomejameswoods/Flickr, 105 (top); Lisa Cardoza Routh/Shutterstock, 105 (bottom); Randy Bjorklund/Shutterstock, 106 (top); NatureDiver/Shutterstock, 106 (bottom); C S Perry Jr/Shutterstock, 107 (top); stillhope/Shutterstock, 107 (bottom)

ABDOBOOKS.COM
Published by Abdo Reference, a division of ABDO, PO Box 398166, Minneapolis, Minnesota 55439.

Printed in China.
102024
012025

Editor: Jane Katirgis
Series Designer: Colleen McLaren

Library of Congress Control Number: 2024938346
Publisher's Cataloging-in-Publication Data
Names: Snow, Peggy, author.
Title: Seashells / by Peggy Snow
Description: Minneapolis, Minnesota : Abdo Reference, 2025 | Series: North American field guides | Includes online resources and index.
Identifiers: ISBN 9781098296179 (lib. bdg.) | ISBN 9798384917175 (ebook)
Subjects: LCSH: Sea shells--Juvenile literature. | Mollusks--Juvenile literature. | Shellfish--Juvenile literature. | Shells--Juvenile literature. | Ecological science--Juvenile literature.
Classification: DDC 594.147--dc23